Treasures from the Spiritual Classics

A SERIOUS CALL TO A DEVOUT AND HOLY LIFE

by

WILLIAM LAW

Compiled by
Roger L. Roberts

Morehouse-Barlow Co., Inc.
Wilton, Connecticut

P9-DTM-149

First USA edition published 1982
Morehouse-Barlow Co., Inc.
78 Danbury Road
Wilton, Connecticut 06897

Printed in the United States of America

PREFACE

The following passages are taken from one of the most famous of all spiritual treatises to have been written in the Church of England through its long history.

William Law was born at Kings Cliffe, Northamptonshire, in 1686 and was educated at Emmanuel College, Cambridge, of which he was elected a Fellow on his ordination in 1711. In 1714, for conscience sake, he refused the Oath of Allegiance to the new Hanoverian sovereign, George I. He thus became one of the Non-jurors and in consequence was deprived both of his Fellowship and of any prospect of preferment in the Church. However, he acquired enormous influence through his writings, the best known of which, the *Serious Call*, was published in 1728 while he was serving as private tutor to the father of the historian Edward Gibbon. In 1740 he returned to his birthplace in Northamptonshire where he lived out the remainder of his life in quiet simplicity, Christian devotion and charitable works until his death in 1761.

The *Serious Call*, as will be evident from these extracts, owed much to the writings of the mediaeval mystics such as Ruysbroek and Thomas à Kempis. But it bears throughout the peculiar stamp of the author's own Anglican genius in its eloquent advocacy of personal devotion to the glory of God and obedience to His will in daily life. Long established as a spiritual classic, the *Serious Call* ranks with Bunyan's Pilgrim's Progress as one of the formative works of English piety.

R.L.R.

The extracts which follow are reprinted from William Law's *A Serious Call to a Devout and Holy Life* edited by Robert F. Horton, and published in 1898 by J. M. Dent and Co.

CHRISTIAN DEVOTION

DEVOTION is neither private nor public prayer; but prayers, whether private or public, are particular parts or instances of devotion. Devotion signifies a life given, or devoted, to God.

He, therefore, is the devout man, who lives no longer to his own will, or the way and spirit of the world, but to the sole will of God; who considers God in everything, who serves God in everything, who makes all the parts of his common life parts of piety, by doing everything in the Name of God, and under such rules as are conformable to His glory.

We readily acknowledge, that God alone is to be the rule and measure of our prayers; that in them we are to look wholly unto Him, and act wholly for Him; that we are only to pray in such a manner, for such things, and such ends, as are suitable to His glory.

Now let any one but find out the reason

why he is to be thus strictly pious in his prayers, and he will find the same as strong a reason to be as strictly pious in all the other parts of his life. For there is not the least shadow of a reason why we should make God the rule and measure of our prayers; why we should then look wholly unto Him, and pray according to His will; but what equally proves it necessary for us to look wholly unto God, and make Him the rule and measure of all the other actions of our life. For any ways of life, any employment of our talents, whether of our parts, our time, or money, that is not strictly according to the will of God, that is not for such ends as are suitable to His glory, are as great absurdities and failings, as prayers that are not according to the will of God. For there is no other reason why our prayers should be according to the will of God, why they should have nothing in them but what is wise, and holy, and heavenly; there is no other reason for this, but that our lives may be of the same nature, full of the same wisdom, holiness, and heavenly tempers, that we may live unto God in the same spirit that we pray unto Him. Were it not our strict duty to live by reason, to devote all the actions of our lives to God, were it not absolutely necessary to walk before Him in wisdom and holiness and all heavenly conversation, doing everything in His Name, and for His glory, there would be no excellency or wisdom in the most heavenly prayers. Nay, such prayers would be absurdities; they would be like prayers for wings, when it was no part of our duty to fly.

As sure, therefore, as there is any wisdom in praying for the Spirit of God, so sure is it, that we are to make that Spirit the rule of all our actions; as sure as it is our duty to look wholly unto God in our prayers, so sure is it that it is our duty to live wholly unto God in our lives. But we can no more be said to live unto God, unless we live unto Him in all the ordinary actions of our life, unless He be the rule and measure of all our ways, than we can be said to pray unto God, unless our prayers look wholly unto Him. So that unreasonable and absurd ways of life, whether in labour or diversion, whether they consume our time, or our money, are like unreasonable and absurd prayers, and are as truly an offence unto God.

It is for want of knowing, or at least considering this, that we see such a mixture of ridicule in the lives of many people. You see them strict as to some times and places of devotion, but when the service of the Church is over, they are but like those that seldom or never come there. In their way of life, their manner of spending their time and money, in their cares and fears, in their pleasures and indulgences, in their labour and diversions, they are like the rest of the world. This makes the loose part of the world generally make a jest of those that are devout, because they see their devotion goes no farther than their prayers, and that when they are over, they live no more unto God, till the time of prayer returns again; but live by the same humour and fancy, and in as full an enjoyment of all the follies of life as other people. This is the reason why they are the jest and scorn of careless and worldly people; not because they are really devoted to God, but because they appear to have no other devotion but that of occasional prayers.

The short of the matter is this; either reason and religion prescribe rules and ends to all the ordinary actions of our life, or they do not: if they do, then it is as necessary to govern all our actions by those rules, as it is necessary to worship God. For if religion teaches us anything concerning eating and drinking, or spending our time and money; if it teaches us how we are to use and contemn the world; if it tells us what tempers we are to have in common life, how we are to be disposed towards all people; how we are to behave towards the sick, the poor, the old, the destitute; if it tells us whom we are to treat with a particular love, whom we are to regard with a particular esteem; if it tells us how we are to treat our enemies, and how we are to mortify and deny ourselves; he must be very weak that can think these parts of religion are not to be observed with as much exactness, as any doctrines that relate to prayers.

ALL THINGS ARE GOD'S

I shall now descend to some particulars, and show how we are to devote our labour and employment, our time and fortunes, unto God.

As a good Christian should consider every place as holy, because God is there, so he should look upon every part of his life as a matter of holiness, because it is to be offered unto God.

The profession of a clergyman is an holy profession, because it is a ministration in holy things, an attendance at the altar. But worldly business is to be made holy unto the Lord, by being done as a service to Him, and in conformity to His Divine will.

For as all men, and all things in the world, as truly belong unto God, as any places, things, or persons, that are devoted to Divine service, so all things are to be used, and all persons are to act in their several states and employments, for the glory of God.

Men of worldly business, therefore, must not look upon themselves as at liberty to live to themselves, to sacrifice to their own humours and tempers, because their employment is of a worldly nature. But they must consider, that, as the world and all worldly professions as truly belong to God, as persons and things that are devoted to the altar, so it is as much the duty of men in worldly business to live wholly unto God, as it is the duty of those who are devoted to Divine service.

As the whole world is God's, so the whole world is to act for God. As all men have the same relation to God, as all men have all their powers and faculties from God, so all men are obliged to act for God, with all their powers and faculties.

As all things are God's, so all things are to be used and regarded as the things of God. For men to abuse things on earth, and live to themselves, is the same rebellion against God, as for angels to abuse things in Heaven; because God is just the same Lord of all on earth, as He is the Lord of all in Heaven.

Things may, and must differ in their use, but yet they are all to be used according to the will of God.

Men may, and must differ in their employments, but yet they must all act for the same ends, as dutiful servants of God, in the right and pious performance of their several callings.

Clergymen must live wholly unto God in one particular way, that is, in the exercise of holy offices, in the ministration of prayers and Sacraments, and a zealous distribution of spiritual goods.

But men of other employments are, in their particular ways, as much obliged to act as the servants of God, and live wholly unto Him

14

in their several callings.

This is the only difference between clergymen and people of other callings.

When it can be shown, that men might be vain, covetous, sensual, worldly-minded, or proud in the exercise of their worldly business, then it will be allowable for clergymen to indulge the same tempers in their sacred profession. For though these tempers are most odious and most criminal in clergymen, who besides their baptismal vow, have a second time devoted themselves to God, to be His servants, not in the common offices of human life, but in the spiritual service of the most holy sacred things, and who are therefore to keep themselves as separate and different from the common life of other men, as a church or an altar is to be kept separate from houses and tables of common use; yet as all Christians are by their Baptism devoted to God, and made professors of holiness, so are they all in their several callings to live as holy and heavenly persons; doing every thing in their common life only in such a manner, as it may be received by God, as a service done to Him. For things spiritual and temporal, sacred and common, must, like men and angels, like Heaven and earth, all conspire in the glory of God.

As there is but one God and Father of us all, whose glory gives light and life to everything that lives, whose presence fills all places, whose power supports all beings, whose providence ruleth all events; so everything that lives, whether in Heaven or earth, whether they be thrones or principalities, men or angels, they must all, with one spirit, live wholly to the praise and glory of this one God and Father of them all. Angels as angels, in their heavenly ministrations; but men as men, women as women, bishops as bishops, priests as priests, and deacons as deacons; some with things spiritual, and some with things temporal, offering to God the daily sacrifice of a reasonable life, wise actions, purity of heart, and heavenly affections.

This is the common business of all persons in this world.

PRAYER AND PRACTICE

He that has appointed times for the use of wise and pious prayers, performs a proper instance of devotion; but he that allows himself no times, nor any places, nor any actions, but such as are strictly conformable to wisdom and holiness, worships the Divine nature with the most true and substantial devotion. For who does not know, that it is better to be pure and holy, than to talk about purity and holiness? Nay, who does not know, that a man is to be reckoned no farther pure, or holy, or just, than as he is pure, and holy, and just in the common course of his life? But if this be plain, then it is also plain, that it is better to be holy, than to have holy prayers.

Prayers, therefore, are so far from being a sufficient devotion, that they are the smallest parts of it. We are to praise God with words and prayers, because it is a possible way of glorifying God, who has given us such faculties, as may be so used. But then as words are but small things in themselves, as times of prayer are but little, if compared with the rest of our lives; so that devotion which consists in times and forms of prayer is but a very small thing, if compared to that devotion which is to appear in every other part and circumstance of our lives.

Again: as it is an easy thing to worship God with forms of words, and to observe times of offering them unto Him, so it is the smallest kind of piety. And, on the other hand, as it is more difficult to worship God with our substance, to honour Him with the right use of our time, to offer to Him the continual sacrifice of self-denial and mortification; as it requires more piety to eat and drink only for such ends as may glorify God, to undertake no labour, nor allow of any diversion, but where we can act in the Name of God; as it is more difficult to sacrifice all our corrupt tempers, correct all our passions, and make piety to God the rule and measure of all the actions of our common life; so the devotion of this kind is a much more acceptable service unto God, than those words of devotion which we offer to Him either in the Church or in our closet.

Every sober reader will easily perceive that I do not intend to lessen the true and great value of prayers, either public or private; but only to show him that they are certainly but a very slender part of devotion, when compared to a devout life.

To see this in a yet clearer light, let us suppose a person to have appointed times for praising God with psalms and hymns, and to be strict in the observation of them; let it be supposed, also, that in his common life he is restless and uneasy, full of murmurings and complaints at every thing, never pleased but by chance, as his temper happens to carry him, but murmuring and repining at the very seasons, and having something to dislike in every thing that happens to him. Now, can you conceive any thing more absurd and unreasonable than such a character as this? Is such a one to be reckoned thankful to God, because he has forms of praise which he offers to Him? Nay, is it not certain that such forms of praise must be so far from being an acceptable devotion to God, that they must be abhorred as an abomination? Now the absurdity which you see in this instance, is the same in any other part of our life; if our common life hath any contrariety to our prayers, it is the same abomination as songs of thanksgiving in the mouths of murmurers.

Bended knees, whilst you are clothed with pride; heavenly petitions, whilst you are hoarding up treasures upon earth; holy devotions, whilst you live in the follies of the world; prayers of meekness and charity, whilst your heart is the seat of spite and resentment; hours of prayer, whilst you give up days and years to idle diversions, impertinent visits, and foolish pleasures; are as absurd, unacceptable services to God, as forms of thanksgiving from a person that lives in re-pinings and discontent.

So that, unless the common course of our lives be according to the common spirit of our prayers, our prayers are so far from being a real or sufficient degree of devotion, that they become an empty lip-labour, or, what is worse, a notorious hypocrisy.

Seeing, therefore, we are to make the spirit and temper of our prayers the common spirit and temper of our lives, this may serve to convince us that all orders of people are to labour and aspire after the same utmost per-fection of the Christian life. For as all Christ-ians are to use the same holy and heavenly devotions, as they are all with the same ear-nestness to pray for the Spirit of God, so is it a sufficient proof that all orders of people are, to the utmost of their power, to make their life agreeable to that one Spirit, for which they are all to pray.

All men, therefore, as men, have one and

the same important business, to act up to the excellency of their rational nature, and to make reason and order the law of all their designs and actions. All Christians, as Christians, have one and the same calling, to live according to the excellency of the Christian spirit, and to make the sublime precepts of the Gospel the rule and measure of all their tempers in common life. The one thing needful to one, is the one thing needful to all.

THE SECRET OF HAPPINESS

Some people will perhaps object, that all these rules of holy living unto God in all that we do, are too great a restraint upon human life; that it will be made too anxious a state, by thus introducing a regard to God in all our actions; and that by depriving ourselves of so many seemingly innocent pleasures, we shall render our lives dull, uneasy, and melancholy.

To which it may be answered,

First, That these rules are prescribed for,

and will certainly procure a quite contrary end. That instead of making our lives dull and melancholy, they will render them full of content and strong satisfactions. That by these rules, we only change the childish satisfactions of our vain and sickly passions, for the solid enjoyments and real happiness of a sound mind.

Secondly, That as there is no foundation for comfort in the enjoyments of this life, but in the assurance that a wise and good God governeth the world, so the more we find out God in every thing, the more we apply to Him in every place, the more we look up to Him in all our actions, the more we conform to His will, the more we act according to His wisdom, and imitate His goodness, by so much the more do we enjoy God, partake of the Divine nature, and heighten and increase all that is happy and comfortable in human life.

Thirdly, He that is endeavouring to subdue, and root out of his mind, all those passions of pride, envy, and ambition, which religion opposes, is doing more to make himself happy, even in this life, than he that is contriving means to indulge them. For these passions are the causes of all the disquiets and vexations of human life: they are the dropsies and fevers of our minds, vexing them with false appetites, and restless cravings after such things as we do not want, and spoiling our taste for those things which are our proper good.

Do but imagine that you somewhere or other saw a man that proposed reason as the rule of all his actions; that had no desires but after such things as nature wants, and religion approves; that was as pure from all the motions of pride, envy, and covetousness, as from thoughts of murder; that, in this freedom from worldly passions, he had a soul full of Divine love, wishing and praying that all men may have what they want of worldly things, and be partakers of eternal glory in the life to come. Do but fancy a man living in this manner, and your own conscience will immediately tell you, that he is the happiest man in the world, and that it is not in the power of the richest fancy to invent any higher happiness in the present state of life.

And, on the other hand, if you suppose him to be in any degree less perfect; if you suppose him but subject to one foolish fondness or vain passion, your own conscience will again tell you that he so far lessens his own happiness, and robs himself of the true enjoyment of his other virtues. So true is it, that the more we live by the rules of religion, the more peaceful and happy do we render our lives.

Again; as it thus appears that real happiness is only to be had from the greatest degrees of piety, the greatest denials of our passions, and the strictest rules of religion; so the same truth will appear from a consideration of human misery. If we look into the world, and view the disquiets and troubles of human life, we shall find that they are all owing to our violent and irreligious passions.

Now all trouble and uneasiness is founded in the want of something or other: would we, therefore, know the true cause of our troubles and disquiets, we must find out the cause of our wants; because that which creates and increaseth our wants, does, in the same degree, create and increase our troubles and disquiets.

God Almighty has sent us into the world with very few wants; meat, and drink, and clothing, are the only things necessary in life; and as these are only our present needs, so the present world is well furnished to supply these needs.

If a man had half the world in his power, he can make no more of it than this; as he wants it only to support an animal life, so is it unable to do any thing else for him, or to afford him any other happiness.

This is the state of man,—born with few wants, and into a large world very capable of supplying them. So that one would reasonably suppose that men should pass their lives in content and thankfulness to God; at least, that they should be free from violent disquiets and vexations, as being placed in a world that has more than enough to relieve all their wants.

But if to all this we add, that this short life, thus furnished with all that we want in it, is only a short passage to eternal glory, where we shall be clothed with the brightness of Angels, and enter into the joys of God, we might still more reasonably expect that human life should be a state of peace, and joy, and delight in God. Thus it would certainly be, if reason had its full power over us.

MAN'S ETERNAL DESTINY

If a man had five fixed years to live, he could not possibly think at all, without intending to make the best use of them all. When he saw his stay so short in this world, he must needs think that this was not a world for him; and when he saw how near he was to another world that was eternal, he must surely think it very necessary to be very diligent in preparing himself for it.

Now as reasonable as piety appears in such a circumstance of life, it is yet more reasonable in every circumstance of life, to every thinking man.

For, who but a madman can reckon that he has five years certain to come?

And if it be reasonable and necessary to deny our worldly tempers, and live wholly unto God, because we are certain that we are to die at the end of five years; surely it must be much more reasonable and necessary for us to live in the same spirit, because we have no certainty that we shall live five weeks.

Again, if we were to add twenty years to the five, which is in all probability more than will be added to the lives of many people, who are at man's estate; what a poor thing is this! how small a difference is there between five and twenty-five years!

It is said, that a day is with God as a thousand years, and a thousand years as one day; because, in regard to His eternity, this difference is as nothing.

Now as we are all created to be eternal, to live in an endless succession of ages upon ages, where thousands, and millions of thousands of years will have no proportion to our everlasting life in God: so with regard to this eternal state, which is our real state, twenty-five years is as poor a pittance as twenty-five days.

Now we can never make any true judgment of time as it relates to us, without considering the true state of our duration. If we are temporary beings, then a little time may justly be called a great deal in relation to us; but if we are eternal beings, then the difference of a few years is as nothing.

If we were to suppose three different sorts of rational beings, all of different, but fixed duration, one sort that lived certainly only a month, the other a year, and the third a hundred years. Now if these beings were to meet together, and talk about time, they must talk in a very different language: half an hour to those that were to live but a month, must be a very different thing to what it is to those who are to live a hundred years.

As, therefore, time is thus different a thing with regard to the state of those who enjoy it, so if we would know what time is with regard to ourselves, we must consider our state.

Now since our eternal state is as certainly ours, as our present state; since we are as certainly to live for ever, as we now live at all; it is plain, that we cannot judge of the value of any particular time, as to us, but by comparing it to that eternal duration, for which we are created.

If you would know what five years signify to a being that was to live a hundred, you must compare five to a hundred, and see what proportion it bears to it; and then you will judge right.

So if you would know what twenty years signify to a son of Adam, you must compare it not to a million of ages, but to an eternal duration, to which no number of millions bears any proportion; and then you will judge right, by finding it nothing.

Consider therefore this; how would you condemn the folly of a man, that should lose his share of future glory, for the sake of being rich, or great, or praised, or delighted in any enjoyment, only one poor day before he was to die!

But if the time will come, when a number of years will seem less to everyone, than a day does now, what a condemnation must it then be, if eternal happiness should appear to be lost for something less than the enjoyment of a day!

Why does a day seem a trifle to us now? It is because we have years to set against it. It is the duration of years that makes it appear as nothing.

What a trifle therefore must the years of a

man's age appear, when they are forced to be set against eternity, when there shall be nothing but eternity to compare them with!

Now this will be the case of every man, as soon as he is out of the body; he will be forced to forget the distinctions of days and years, and to measure time, not by the course of the sun, but by setting it against eternity.

As the fixed stars, by reason of our being placed at such a distance from them, appear but as so many points; so when we, placed in eternity, shall look back upon all time, it will all appear but as a moment.

Then, a luxury, an indulgence, a prosperity, a greatness of fifty years, will seem to every one that looks back upon it, as the same poor short enjoyment as if he had been snatched away in his first sin.

These few reflections upon time are only to show how poorly they think, how miserably they judge, who are less careful of an eternal state, because they may be at some years' distance from it, than they would be if they knew they were within a few weeks of it.

PRIVATE PRAYER

All people that have ever made any reflections upon what passes in their own hearts, must know that they are mighty changeable in regard to devotion. Sometimes our hearts are so awakened, have such strong apprehensions of the Divine Presence, are so full of deep compunction for our sins, that we cannot confess them in any language but that of tears.

Sometimes the light of God's countenance shines so bright upon us, we see so far into the invisible world, we are so affected with the wonders of the love and goodness of God, that our hearts worship and adore in a language higher than that of words, and we feel transports of devotion, which only can be felt.

On the other hand, sometimes we are so sunk into our bodies, so dull and unaffected with that which concerns our souls, that our hearts are as much too low for our prayers; we cannot keep pace with our forms of confession, or feel half of that in our hearts which we have in our mouths; we thank and praise God with forms of words, but our hearts have little or no share in them.

It is therefore highly necessary to provide against this inconstancy of our hearts, by having at hand such forms of prayer as may best suit us when our hearts are in their best state, and also be most likely to raise and stir them up when they are sunk into dulness. For, as words have a power of affecting our hearts on all occasions, as the same thing differently expressed has different effects upon our minds, so it is reasonable that we should make this advantage of language, and provide ourselves with such forms of expression as are most likely to move and enliven our souls, and fill them with sentiments suitable to them.

The first thing that you are to do, when you are upon your knees, is to shut your eyes, and with a short silence let your soul place itself in the presence of God; that is, you are to use this, or some other better method, to separate yourself from all common thoughts, and make your heart as sensible as you can of the Divine presence.

Now if this recollection of spirit is necessary,—as who can say it is not?—then how poorly must they perform their devotions, who are always in a hurry; who begin them in haste, and hardly allow themselves time to repeat their very form, with any gravity or attention! Theirs is properly saying prayers, instead of praying.

To proceed: if you were to use yourself (as far as you can) to pray always in the same place; if you were to reserve that place for devotion, and not allow yourself to do any thing common in it; if you were never to be there yourself, but in times of devotion; if any little room, or (if that cannot be) if any particular part of a room was thus used, this kind of consecration of it as a place holy unto God, would have an effect upon your mind, and dispose you to such tempers, as would very much assist your devotion. For by having a place thus sacred in your room, it would in some measure resemble a chapel or house of God. This would dispose you to be always in the spirit of religion, when you were there; and fill you with wise and holy thoughts, when you were by yourself. Your own apartment would raise in your mind such sentiments as you have when you stand near an altar; and you would be afraid of thinking or doing any thing that was foolish near that place, which is the place of prayer and holy intercourse with God.

When you begin your petitions, use such various expressions of the attributes of God, as may make you most sensible of the greatness and power of the Divine Nature.

Begin, therefore, in words like these: O Being of all beings, Fountain of all light and glory, gracious Father of men and Angels, whose universal Spirit is everywhere present, giving life, and light, and joy, to all Angels in

Heaven, and all creatures upon earth, etc.

For these representations of the Divine attributes, which show us in some degree the Majesty and greatness of God, are an excellent means of raising our hearts into lively acts of worship and adoration.

Although, therefore, prayer does not consist in fine words, or studied expressions; yet as words speak to the soul, as they have a certain power of raising thoughts in the soul; so those words which speak of God in the highest manner, which most fully express the power and presence of God, which raise thoughts in the soul most suitable to the greatness and providence of God, are the most useful and most edifying in our prayers.

When you direct any of your petitions to our blessed Lord, let it be in some expressions of this kind: O Saviour of the world, God of God, Light of Light; Thou that art the brightness of Thy Father's glory, and the express Image of His Person; Thou that art the Alpha and Omega, the Beginning and End of all things; Thou that hast destroyed the power of the devil; that hast overcome death; Thou that art entered into the Holy of Holies, that sittest at the right hand of the Father, that art high above all thrones and principalities, that makest intercession for all the world; Thou that art the Judge of the quick and dead; Thou that wilt speedily come down in Thy Father's glory, to reward all men according to their works, be Thou my Light and my Peace, etc.

For such representations, which describe so many characters of our Saviour's nature and power, are not only proper acts of adoration, but will, if they are repeated with any attention, fill our hearts with the highest fervours of true devotion.

CONQUEST OF THE WORLD

The history of the Gospel is chiefly the history of Christ's conquest over the spirit of the world. And the number of true Christians is only the number of those who, following the

Spirit of Christ, have lived contrary to this spirit of the world.

"If any man hath not the Spirit of Christ, he is none of His." Again, "Whatsoever is born of God, overcometh the world." "Set your affection on things above, and not on things on the earth; for ye are dead, and your life is hid with Christ in God." This is the language of the whole New Testament: this is the mark of Christianity: you are to be dead, that is, dead to the spirit and temper of the world, and live a new life in the Spirit of Jesus Christ.

But notwithstanding the clearness and plainness of these doctrines which thus renounce the world, yet great part of Christians live and die slaves to the customs and temper of the world.

How many people swell with pride and vanity, for such things as they would not know how to value at all, but that they are admired in the world!

Would a man take ten years more drudgery

in business to add two horses more to his coach, but that he knows that the world most of all admires a coach and six? How fearful are many people of having their houses poorly furnished, or themselves meanly clothed, for this only reason, lest the world should make no account of them, and place them amongst low and mean people!

How often would a man have yielded to the haughtiness and ill-nature of others, and shown a submissive temper, but that he dares not pass for such a poor-spirited man in the opinion of the world!

Many a man would often drop a resentment, and forgive an affront, but that he is afraid if he should, the world would not forgive him.

How many would practise Christian temperance and sobriety, in its utmost perfection, were it not for the censure which the world passes upon such a life!

Others have frequent intentions of living up to the rules of Christian perfection, which they are frighted from by considering what the world would say of them.

Thus do the impressions which we have received from living in the world enslave our minds, that we dare not attempt to be eminent in the sight of God and holy angels, for fear of being little in the eyes of the world.

From this quarter arises the greatest difficulty of humility, because it cannot subsist in any mind, but so far as it is dead to the world, and has parted with all desires of enjoying its greatness and honours. So that in order to be truly humble, you must unlearn all those notions which you have been all your life learning from this corrupt spirit of the world.

You can make no stand against the assaults of pride, the meek affections of humility can have no place in your soul, till you stop the power of the world over you, and resolve against a blind obedience to its laws.

The Christian's great conquest over the world is all contained in the mystery of Christ upon the Cross. It was there, and from thence, that He taught all Christians how they were to come out of, and conquer the world, and what they were to do in order to be His disciples. And all the doctrines, Sacraments, and institutions of the Gospel are only so many explications of the meaning, and applications of the benefit, of this great mystery.

And the state of Christianity implieth nothing else, but an entire, absolute conformity to that spirit which Christ showed in the mysterious Sacrifice of Himself upon the Cross.

Every man therefore is only so far a Christian, as he partakes of this Spirit of Christ. It was this that made St Paul so passionately express himself, "God forbid that I should glory, save in the cross of our Lord Jesus Christ": but why does he glory? Is it because Christ had suffered in his stead, and had excused him from suffering? No, by no means. But it was because his Christian profession had called him to the honour of suffering with Christ, and of dying to the world under reproach and contempt, as He had done upon the Cross. For he immediately adds, "by whom the world is crucified unto me, and I unto the world." This, you see, was the reason of his glory in the Cross of Christ, because it had called him to a like state of death and crucifixion to the world.

Thus was the Cross of Christ, in St Paul's days, the glory of Christians; not as it signified their not being ashamed to own a Master that was crucified, but as it signified their glorying in a religion which was nothing else but a doctrine of the Cross, that called them to the same suffering spirit, the same sacrifice of themselves, the same renunciation of the world, the same humility and meekness, the same patient bearing of injuries, reproaches, and contempts, and the same dying to all the greatness, honours, and happiness of this world, which Christ showed upon the Cross.

To have a true idea of Christianity, we must not consider our Blessed Lord as suffering in our stead, but as our Representative, acting in our name, and with such particular merit, as to make our joining with Him acceptable unto God.

He suffered, and was a Sacrifice, to make our sufferings and sacrifice of ourselves fit to be received by God. And we are to suffer, to be crucified, to die, and rise with Christ; or else His Crucifixion, Death, and Resurrection, will profit us nothing.

LOVE OF NEIGHBOUR

Now we are to love our neighbour, that is, all mankind, not because they are wise, holy, virtuous, or well-behaved; for all mankind neither ever was, nor ever will be so; therefore it is certain, that the reason of our being obliged to love them cannot be founded in their virtue.

Again; if their virtue or goodness were the reason of our being obliged to love people, we should have no rule to proceed by; because though some people's virtues or vices are very notorious, yet, generally speaking, we are but very ill judges of the virtue and merit of other people.

Thirdly, We are sure that the virtue or merit of persons is not the reason of our being obliged to love them, because we are commanded to pay the highest instances of love to our worst enemies; we are to love, and bless, and pray for those that most injuriously treat us. This therefore is demonstration, that the merit of persons is not the reason on which our obligation to love them is founded.

Let us farther consider, what that love is which we owe to our neighbour. It is to love him as ourselves, that is, to have all those sentiments towards him which we have towards ourselves; to wish him everything that we may lawfully wish to ourselves; to be glad of every good, and sorry for every evil, that happens to him; and to be ready to do him all such acts of kindness, as we are always ready to do to ourselves.

This love, therefore, you see, is nothing

else but a love of benevolence; it requires nothing of us but such good wishes, tender affections, and such acts of kindness, as we show to ourselves.

This is all the love that we owe to the best of men; and we are never to want any degree of this love to the worst or most unreasonable man in the world.

Now what is the reason why we are to love every man in this manner? It is answered that our obligation to love all men in this manner is founded upon many reasons.

First, Upon a reason of equity; for if it is just to love ourselves in this manner, it must be unjust to deny any degree of this love to others, because every man is so exactly of the same nature, and in the same condition as ourselves.

If, therefore, your own crimes and follies do not lessen your obligation to seek your own good, and wish well to yourself; neither do the follies and crimes of your neighbour lessen your obligation to wish and seek the good of your neighbour.

Another reason for this love is founded in the authority of God, who has commanded us to love every man as ourself.

Thirdly, We are obliged to this love in imitation of God's goodness, that we may be children of our Father which is in Heaven, who willeth the happiness of all His creatures, and maketh his sun to rise on the evil, and on the good.

Fourthly, Our redemption by Jesus Christ calleth us to the exercise of this love, who came from Heaven and laid down His life, out of love to the whole sinful world.

Fifthly, By the command of our Lord and Saviour, who has required us to love one another, as He has loved us.

These are the great, perpetual reasons, on which our obligation to love all mankind as ourselves is founded.

These reasons never vary or change, they always continue in the full force; and therefore equally oblige at all times, and in regard to all persons.

God loves us, not because we are wise, and good, and holy, but in pity to us, because we want this happiness: He loves us, in order to make us good. Our love, therefore, must take this course; not looking for, or requiring the merit of our brethren, but pitying their disorders, and wishing them all the good that they want and are capable of receiving.

It appears now plainly, from what has been said, that the love which we owe to our brethren, is only a love of benevolence. Secondly, That this duty of benevolence is founded upon such reasons as never vary or change, such as have no dependence upon the qualities of persons. From whence it follows that it is the same great sin, to want this love to a bad man, as to want it to a good man. Because he that denies any of this benevolence to a bad man, offends against all the same reasons of love, as he does that denies any benevolence to a good man; and consequently it is the same sin.

When, therefore, you let loose any ill-natured passion, either of hatred or contempt towards (as you suppose) an ill man, consider what you would think of another that was doing the same towards a good man, and be assured that you are committing the same sin.

The whole of the matter is this. The actions which you are to love, esteem, and admire, are the actions of good and pious men; but the persons to whom you are to do all the good you can, in all sorts of kindness and compassion, are all persons, whether good or bad.

INTERCESSION

This was the ancient friendship of Christians, uniting and cementing their hearts, not by worldly considerations, or human passions, but by the mutual communication of spiritual blessings, by prayers and thanksgivings to God for one another.

It was this holy intercession that raised

Christians to such a state of mutual love, as far exceeded all that had been praised and admired in human friendship. And when the same spirit of intercession is again in the world, when Christianity has the same power over the hearts of people that it then had, this holy friendship will be again in fashion, and Christians will be again the wonder of the world, for that exceeding love which they bear to one another.

For a frequent intercession with God, earnestly beseeching Him to forgive the sins of all mankind, to bless them with His providence, enlighten them with His Spirit, and bring them to everlasting happiness, is the divinest exercise that the heart of man can be engaged in.

Be daily, therefore, on your knees, in a solemn deliberate performance of this devotion, praying for others in such forms, with such length, importunity, and earnestness, as you use for yourself; and you will find all little, ill-natured passions die away, your heart grow great and generous, delighting in the common happiness of others, as you used only to delight in your own.

For he that daily prays to God, that all men may be happy in Heaven, takes the likeliest way to make him wish for, and delight in their happiness on earth. And it is hardly possible for you to beseech and entreat God to make any one happy in the highest enjoyments of his glory to all eternity, and yet be troubled to see him enjoy the much smaller gifts of God in this short and low state of human life.

For how strange and unnatural would it be, to pray to God to grant health and a longer life to a sick man, and at the same time to envy him the poor pleasure of agreeable medicines!

Yet this would be no more strange or unnatural than to pray to God that your neighbour may enjoy the highest degrees of His mercy and favour, and yet at the same time envy him the little credit and figure he hath amongst his fellow-creatures.

When therefore you have once habituated your heart to a serious performance of this holy intercession, you have done a great deal to render it incapable of spite and envy, and to make it naturally delight in the happiness of all mankind.

This is the natural effect of a general intercession for all mankind. But the greatest benefits of it are then received, when it descends to such particular instances as our state and condition in life more particularly require of us.

Though we are to treat all mankind as neighbours and brethren, as any occasion offers; yet as we can only live in the actual society of a few, and are by our state and condition more particularly related to some than others; so when our intercession is made an exercise of love and care for those amongst whom our lot is fallen, or who belong to us in a nearer relation, it then becomes the greatest benefit to ourselves, and produces its best effects in our own hearts.

If therefore you should always change and alter your intercessions, according as the needs and necessities of your neighbours or acquaintance seem to require; beseeching God to deliver them from such or such particular evils, or to grant them this or that particular gift, or blessing; such intercessions, besides the great charity of them, would have a mighty effect upon your own heart, as disposing you to every other good office, and to the exercise of every other virtue towards such persons, as have so often a place in your prayers.

This would make it pleasant to you to be courteous, civil, and condescending to all about you; and make you unable to say or do a rude or hard thing to those, for whom you had used yourself to be so kind and compassionate in your prayers.

For there is nothing that makes us love a man so much as praying for him; and when you can once do this sincerely for any man, you have fitted your soul for the performance of everything that is kind and civil towards him. This will fill your heart with a generosity and tenderness, that will give you a better and sweeter behaviour than anything that is called fine breeding and good manners.

By considering yourself as an advocate with God for your neighbours and acquaintance, you would never find it hard to be at peace with them yourself. It would be easy to you to bear with and forgive those, for whom you particularly implored the Divine mercy and forgiveness.

Such prayers as these amongst neighbours and acquaintance, would unite them to one another in the strongest bonds of love and tenderness. It would exalt and ennoble their souls, and teach them to consider one another in a higher state, as members of a spiritual society, that are created for the enjoyment of the common blessings of God, and fellow-heirs of the same future glory.

And by being thus desirous that every one

should have his full share of the favours of God, they would not only be content, but glad to see one another happy in the little enjoyments of this transitory life.

These would be the natural effects of such an intercession, amongst people of the same town or neighbourhood, or that were acquainted with one another's state and condition.

WORSHIP OF GOD

For if there is an infinitely wise and good Creator, in whom we live, move, and have our being, whose providence governs all things in all places, surely it must be the highest act of our understanding to conceive rightly of Him; it must be the noblest instance of judgment, the most exalted temper of our nature, to worship and adore this universal providence, to conform to its laws, to study its wisdom, and to live and act everywhere, as in the presence of this infinitely good and wise Creator.

Now he that lives thus, lives in the spirit of devotion.

And what can show such great parts, and so fine an understanding, as to live in this temper?

For if God is wisdom, surely he must be the wisest man in the world, who most conforms to the wisdom of God, who best obeys His providence, who enters farthest into His designs, and does all he can, that God's will may be done on earth, as it is done in Heaven.

A devout man makes a true use of his reason: he sees through the vanity of the world, discovers the corruption of his nature, and the blindness of his passion. He lives by a law which is not visible to vulgar eyes; he enters into the world of spirits; he compares the greatest things, sets eternity against time; and chooses rather to be for ever great in the presence of God, when he dies, than to have the greatest share of worldly pleasure whilst he lives.

He that is devout, is full of these great thoughts; he lives upon these noble reflections, and conducts himself by rules and principles, which can only be apprehended, admired, and loved by reason.

There is nothing therefore that shows so great a genius, nothing that so plainly declares an heroic greatness of mind, as great devotion.

When you suppose a man to be a saint, or all devotion, you have raised him as much above all other conditions of life, as a philosopher is above an animal.

Lastly; courage and bravery are words of a great sound, and seem to signify an heroic spirit; but yet humility, which seems to be the lowest, meanest part of devotion, is a more certain argument of a noble and courageous mind.

For humility contends with greater enemies, is more constantly engaged, more violently assaulted, bears more, suffers more, and requires greater courage to support itself, than any instances of worldly bravery.

A man that dares be poor and contemptible in the eyes of the world, to approve himself to God; that resists and rejects all human glory, that opposes the clamour of his passions, that meekly puts up with all injuries and wrongs, and dares stay for his reward till the invisible hand of God gives to every one their proper places, endures a much greater trial, and exerts a nobler fortitude, than he that is bold and daring in the fire of battle.

For the boldness of a soldier, if he is a stranger to the spirit of devotion, is rather weakness than fortitude; it is at best but mad passion, and heated spirits, and has no more true valour in it than the fury of a tiger.

For as we cannot lift up a hand, or stir a foot, but by a power that is lent us from God; so bold actions that are not directed by the laws of God, as so many executions of His will, are no more true bravery, than sedate malice is Christian patience.

Reason is our universal law, that obliges us in all places, and at all times; and no actions have any honour, but so far as they are instances of our obedience to reason.

And it is as base and cowardly, to be bold and daring against the principle of reason and justice, as to be bold and daring in lying and perjury.

Would we therefore exercise a true fortitude, we must do all in the spirit of devotion, be valiant against the corruptions of the world, and the lusts of the flesh, and the temptations of the devil; for to be daring and courageous against these enemies, is the noblest bravery that an human mind is capable of.

I have made this digression, for the sake of those who think a great devotion to be bigotry and poorness of spirit; that by these considerations they may see, how poor and mean all other tempers are, if compared to it; that they may see, that all worldly attainments, whether of greatness, wisdom, or bravery, are but empty sounds; and there is nothing wise, or great, or noble, in an human spirit, but rightly to know and heartily worship and adore the great God, that is the support and life of all spirits, whether in Heaven or on earth.